I WROTE MY NAME ON THE WALL

269286

TEXT AND
PHOTOGRAPHS BY
RONNI SOLBERT

JOHNSON FREE PUBLIC LIBRARY
HACKENSACK AREA REFERENCE LIB.
HACKENSACK, N.J.

Little, Brown and Company
BOSTON   TORONTO

COPYRIGHT © 1971 BY RONNI SOLBERT

ALL RIGHTS RESERVED. NO PART OF THIS BOOK MAY BE REPRODUCED IN ANY FORM.

LIBRARY OF CONGRESS CATALOG CARD NO. 70-150056

FIRST EDITION

T 09/71

Published simultaneously in Canada
by Little, Brown & Company (Canada) Limited

PRINTED IN THE UNITED STATES OF AMERICA

In memory of Russell "Negrete" Blackwell
and Carl Memling
1969

Pee Wee, Elena, Socorro
and me,
we live in the same house.
The one across the street
with the oil sign.
That's me,
Jesus de Santiago,
in front.

Seem like Rudolph
always goin off
an takin Charlie with him.
No tellin where that dog
lead him.
An sometime
they gone a long while.

They put up this cement wall
and we wrote
our names in it.
All the kids on the block.
I wrote mine
in three different places.
J-O-H-N,
that's me.

Jimmy sells *piraguas*
by the corner all day.
Twelve flavors —
dime a cup.
Jimmy works fast
and don't ever smile.
I like pineapple best.

This game
we call *Caracol.*
That means snail.
In The Islands
we play on hard sand
by the water.
We use snail shells
instead of stones.

Timmy's antitank gun jammed
and he lost all the darts,
so he lets me use it.

Manny give Homer
one of his hound pups.
Homer workin on
learnin Tiger
his name.
Then he gonna
train him
for a watchdog.
Right now he got
little teeth,
but they real pointy.

Our clubhouse
has a secret door
and you got to have
the password
to get in.
We change it
every day.

Sammy's stuck
in the chicken crate
and Lily Wu's scared.
He went inside
and it fell
on the door
so he can't open it.
We got to turn it over
and let him out.

I quit playin shades
with Bingo.
He clean me out
last week,
an now
he workin on Hector.
Bingo play
with one deck
an keep his other
upstairs.

Lunch hour we hang out
at the Pizza King.
Lenny's uncle works there
makin up the pies.
He don't give out nothin free
cept maybe pepper.

Me an Shorty
got a shoeshine set up
on the avenue.
Some days we make out good.
Some days not so good.
Sundays are best.

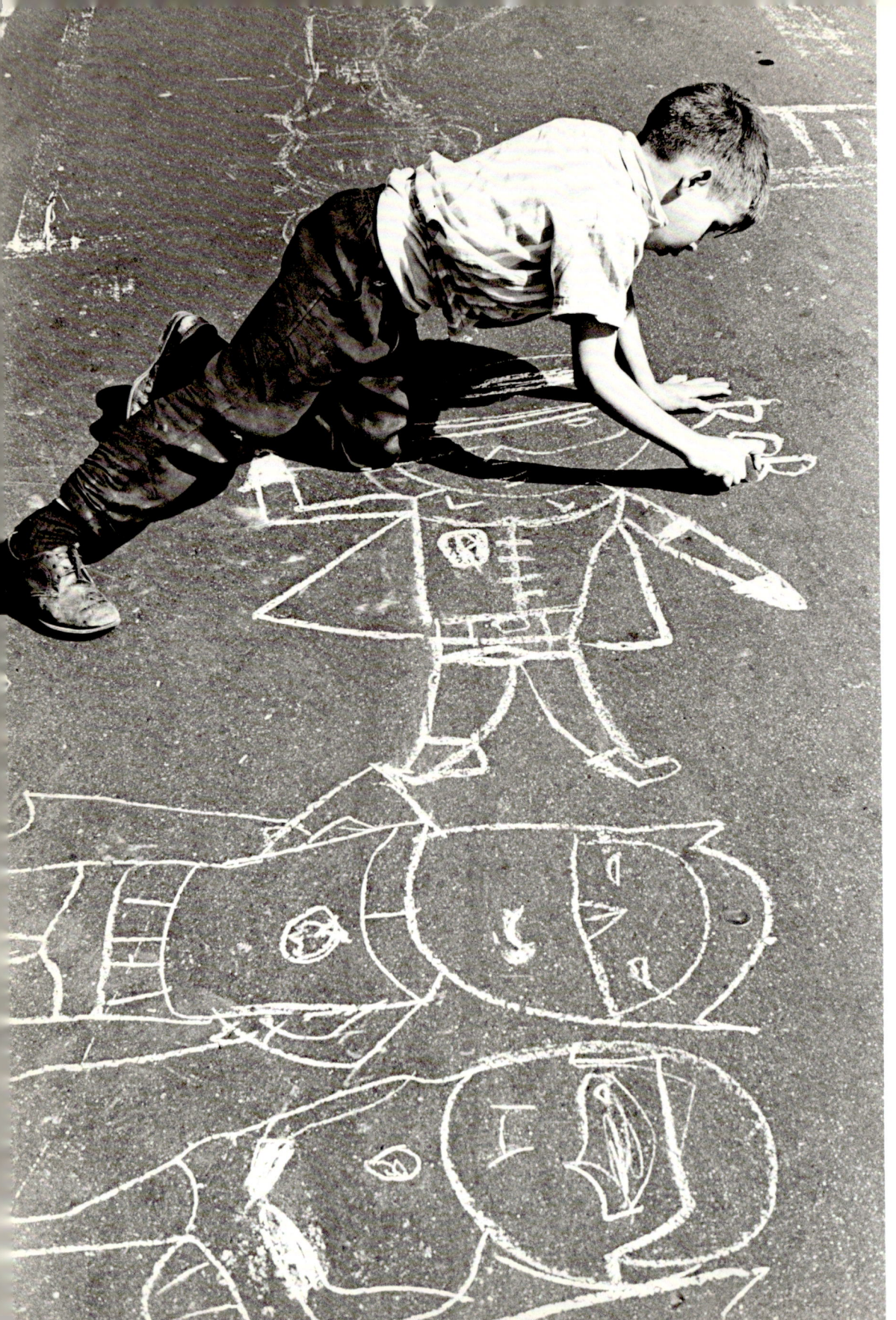

I made two Batmans, and this is R-O-B-I-N. Robin has a zipper in front.

The twins is fixed nice
for Granma.
Monica got to watch
see they don't get mussed
fore she come.
It's hard waitin on company.

The gas company
dug up our street,
so now we got
a real mountain
for war games.

Our block had a fiesta on Saturday.
With a roasted pig
and lots of soda and music and dancing.
Everybody came
and everybody got a chance to turn the pig.

It's hard to fly a kite
in the street.
On the roof
you can't run far
and it gets stuck
down the air shaft

or hung up on TV aerials.

But sometimes,
when there's a big wind,
my kite takes off
higher than pigeons.

We're building in the park
with lots of wood,
big nails and hammers and saws.
Gino and Cowboy made a house
and José fixed a ladder to get in.
We pulled it down before we left
so nobody else would.

We play ball anywhere.
But mostly we play in lots
cause the street's too crowded.
The city said they'd fix a park
in this one.
But that was nine years ago
when my uncle was a kid.

Man, this is crazy!
I see clear across the river
and all the cars on the bridge
and all the people in them.

If I blow
soft,
the bubbles come
big
and pop.

If I blow
hard,
the bubbles come
small
and fly all over.

Take me in your c[art]
huh, Rachel?
We'll go fast
like the boys.
Maybe faster.

Look like Peanut
set to mess with Crazy Joe.
Them two never lets up
hollerin an punchin.
They best friends.

Mira Coco!
El Coco pelado!
Home from the barber
with his new haircut.
Coco pelado!

Rosa,
you gonna
gimme a lick
on your ice, huh —
fore you done?

Mira! Mira!
See our TV show!
Three ladies in boxes.
I sing,
Carla dance,
Mona clap,
an everybody watch.

Eh, Ramón, *ven aquí!*
Your dog's eating the stuffings
outta my snake.
He gonna be
a real live stuffed animal!
Eh, leggo you!

Hold it.
Don't shoot now.
Wait for him to come out.

We seen em,
Papo, too.
They cut through
the schoolyard
and beat it
up the street.

Loretta,
she make that wheel
fly up
an twirl round
an come on back to her.

How she do that?

We go to Dojo
Saturdays,
me an Luis.
We practice every day
for White Belts.

Out here no mats,
so you liable crack a bone
on the ce-ment.

Dig my flyin side-kick!

Melinda an me waitin for the carousel to go. The engine break down an we only get half a ride.

You can't eat cotton candy
without you get sticky all over.
Mine's purple,
an I'm givin Claudie some
so she'll be purple too.

Olé!
Mickey's the wild bull
and me, I'm Pepito Galindo
famous *torero*
making *pases*
in the bullring.
Olé! Olé!

My friend Jim
keeps pigeons
on the roof.
Twenty-three
in a big coop
he built himself.
Jim works nights.
Sometimes he lets me
help him fly
on weekends.
I hold the wand
and make big slow circles
on the sky.
The pigeons all go
round and round.
Except Maxie.
He hates to fly.

Shorty bust his scooter again
and lose all the parts.
Last time I fixed it good.
This time it gonna be a one-wheel job.

I love Mrs. Pentojo's
bride doll.
She sew that dress herself.
My sister Sophie
have a dress like that
for her wedding.
An she have white satin shoes
to go with it.

LeRoi, Timmy and Flo
hidin out by the meat market
under Mama's old umbrella.
They watchin for me
to come round the corner
an I behind the truck
spyin on them.

Carlos give Toto
a haircut
like a Indian.
All shaved
cept on top.
Toto wear his hat
outta school.

There go
Demetrius Hornby Cole.
We calls him Dimmy.
He too little
for that big name
but he give it all
every day at roll call.

Clovell an me waitin on Gladys
for a turn with the bike.
She get it new
when she make her twelfth birthday
an she let us ride
up the block an back.

You gimme back my ball,
you creep,
or man
I bust your head in good!

We has a secret place,
me an Jojo.
Don't no one know
where it's at
an we ain't tellin!

At home
in The Islands
our sand is white and smooth.
We sell it
to people in the town.
It's a day's walk
but they pay high money.

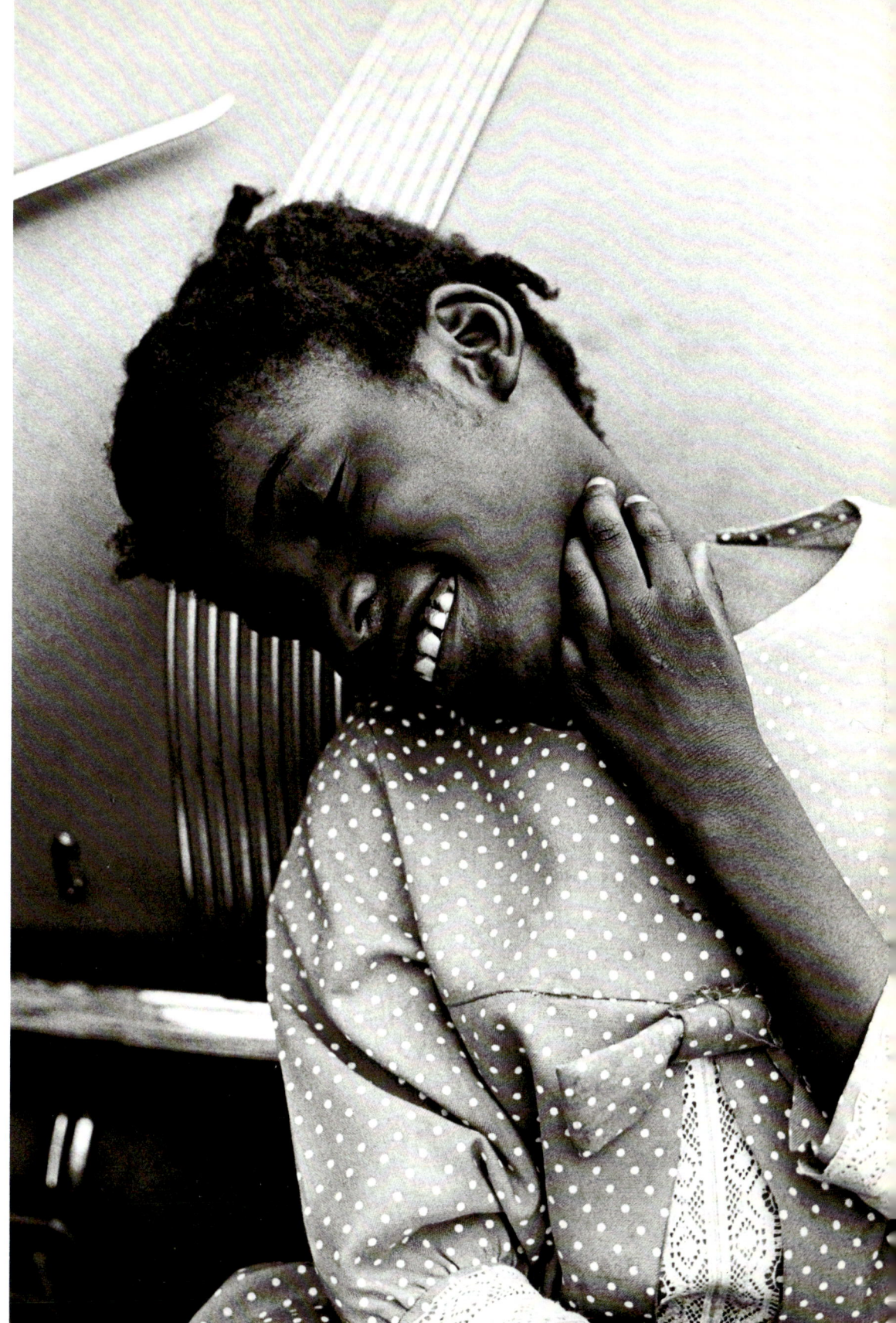

Odetta, she jive you
right outta your skin
if she a mind to.

The pink tree belong to Mr. Olsen.
He have all kind of flowers in there
and he say that tree give real cherries
if we don't pick the blossoms off it.

Che says the stars
been up there
a long long time.
They seen everything
from the first beginning
and they still shining.

Easter morning
we had a big parade
for Peace
all round our block,
with balloons
and everybody singing.

A cop car came out
to watch
and drove in front
all the way.

Josie's at the beauty shop
getting her hair fixed
and Orletta's at the agency
so I got to baby-sit
from now to three.

This lot belongs to us.
To our club.
So does the hole in the fence,
and my dog knows who to keep out
and who to let in.
People are easier to keep out
than garbage.

My sister,
walking or sleeping,
always dreaming.
She claims she meets
real beautiful people dreaming
Anyhow, she smiles a lot.

Sometimes I have
real pretty dreams.
I'm a movie queen
going to a ball
or I'm singing
and dancing on TV
where everyone
can see.

It works
when I'm alone
or dreaming
in my sleep.
But if I see
someone watching,
I remember
I'm me.

When Queenie got run over
by the bus
I buried her
in the lot next door.
Dino said to put a cross
on the grave,
so I did.

Man, if he finds out
we know,
he'll jack us up good.
We better split.

Where I live?
   Up the street
   by the Laundromat.
   Where the sign is.
How long?
   I don't remember.
   We was in the Project before.
My father?
   No. Just me,
   Auntie, Frisco,
   Tina an baby.
School?
   Yeah. P.S. 29 on the corner.
   But Frisco too big
   an too crazy to go.

Lemme be.
You mess with me
an my brother git you.
Man, he lay you out!

This a picture
of my cat Sheba.
And my sister Anita.
Sheba going
to eat her
and she about to holler.

What I see?
What I don't see —
it be there
jus the same.

Yeah, I see em.
They shootin up
an flyin so high
they don't know to cut
fore the cops come.

The pigeon was dead.
They said some kids
were throwing rocks,
but the park was empty.
We made a hole
and buried it in the sandbox.

Sometimes I'm scared
and can't say why.
It comes and goes quick,
and I forget.

Quit buggin me.
I don't know,
and I wouldn't tell anyhow.

A person got a lot of things
all crowded up inside.
Like bein scared
an bein lonely.
All kinds crazy things
an when he get real shook up
no tellin what come out.

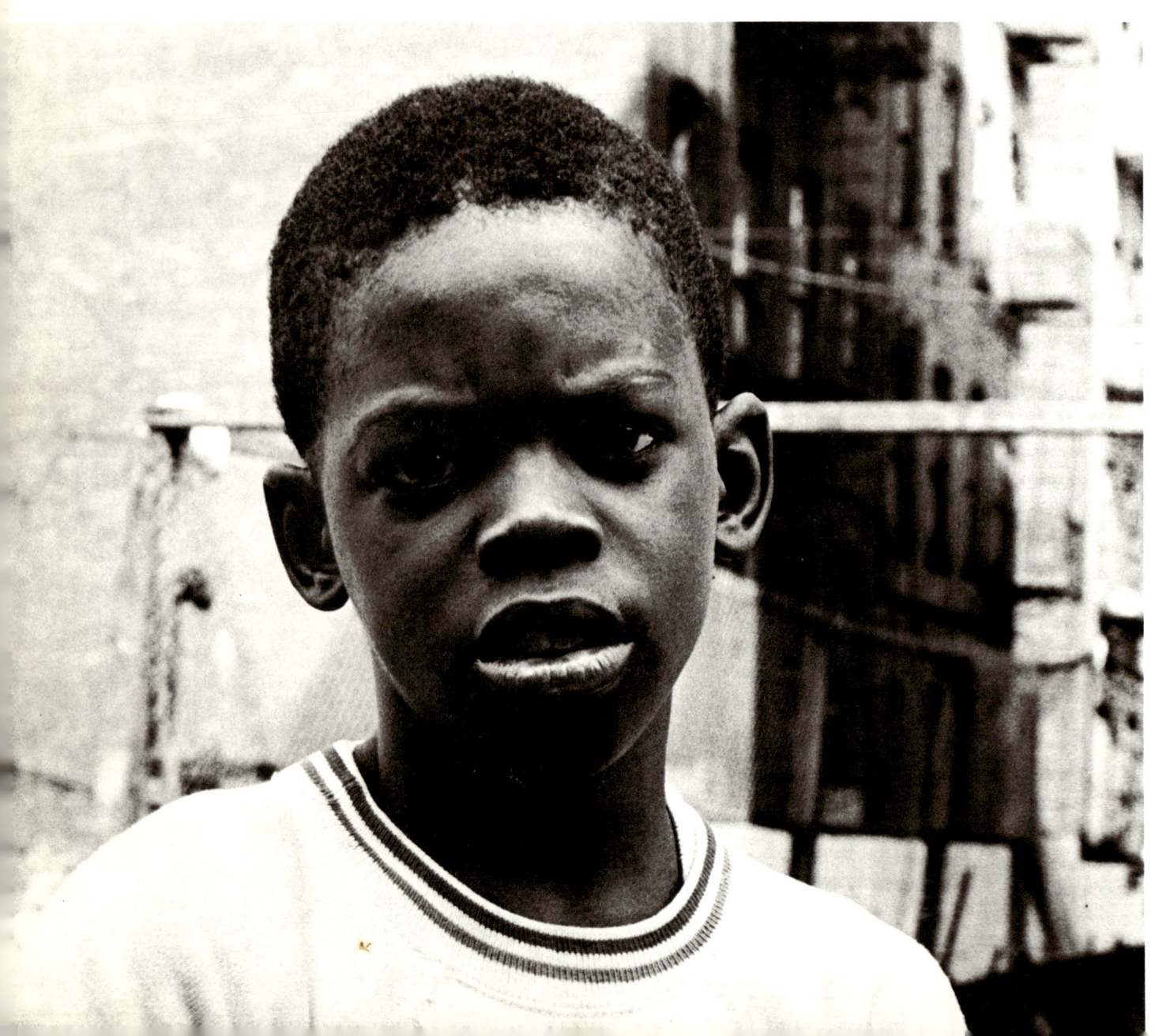

Did you ever
want something
so long
and so bad
you got tired
of it?
I mean
even if someone
gave it to you
you wouldn't
want it
because
it came too late.

Brother,
you cuts me in
now.
I ain't waitin
on no tomorrows!

E811 269286
Solbert 5.95
I wrote my name on the wall.

Johnson Free Public Library
Hackensack, New Jersey